We Pray in Many Ways

written by Christine Way Skinner
illustrations by Céleste Gagnon

Nihil Obstat: Dr. Connie Price, Ph.D.
Censor Deputatus
24 March 2017

Imprimatur: Thomas Cardinal Collins
Archbishop of Toronto
24 March 2017

Twenty-Third Publications
1 Montauk Avenue » Suite 200
New London, CT 06320
(860) 437-3012 » (800) 321-0411
www.twentythirdpublications.com

ISBN: 978-1-62785-197-8

Printed in China.

 A division of Bayard, Inc.

To the people who most inspired me in my vocation: Fr. Bill Burns, Sr. Pauline Lally, SP and Sr. Donna Rose, CND.
~ CWS

To my parents and my sister; without their support, I would not be where I am today.
~ CG

This book belongs to:

_____

My school: _____

My parish: _____

God loves us.
God talks to us and we talk to God.
Talking with God is called PRAYER.

We can pray in many ways!

We have some special prayers that we love so much,
we learn them by heart.
One of them is a prayer that Jesus taught us.

Our Father, who art in heaven,
hallowed be thy name;
thy kingdom come,
thy will be done
on earth as it is in heaven.
Give us this day our daily bread,
and forgive us our trespasses,
as we forgive those who trespass against us;
and lead us not into temptation,
but deliver us from evil. Amen.

Sometimes we pray to Mary, the mother of Jesus.
We ask her to pray for us when we say the Hail Mary.
Part of this prayer comes from the Bible.

Hail Mary,
full of grace,
the Lord is with you.
Blessed are you among women
and blessed is the fruit of your womb, Jesus.
Holy Mary, Mother of God,
pray for us sinners,
now and at the hour of our death. Amen.

We can pray alone.

We can pray with others.

We can be very still and quiet
when we talk to God.

And we can celebrate in joy!

We can sing our prayers

... and dance our prayers

... and write or draw our prayers.

We can use many things
to help us pray.

We can bless ourselves with holy water to remember that we became a member of God's family when we were baptized.

We can bless our homes and our pets and ask God to keep them safe.

We can hang a cross or crucifix in our home
to remember how much Jesus loves us.

We can look at beautiful icons, pictures and statues and remember that God fills our world with beauty.

We can listen to God's word in the Bible
to learn about what God has done for us.

We can travel to faraway places on pilgrimage to hear God's voice ... and we can hear God's voice in our very own bedroom when we are tucked under our cozy blankets.

We can also ask the saints
to pray for us and help us.

St. Francis of Assisi
St. Mother Teresa
St. Marguerite d'Youville
St. Kateri Tekakwitha
St. Ignatius of Loyola
St. Brother André
St. Nicholas of Myra

And we can ask our family and friends
to pray for us. We can pray for them, too!

We can tell God
when we are happy.

We can tell God when
we are sad or confused
or worried or angry.

We can ask God to give us what we need.

But sometimes God's answer will surprise us!

We can say thank you for all the wonderful things God does for us.

Our most important prayer of all is on Sunday, when we gather together for Holy Mass.

There are so many ways to speak
to God and hear God's voice.

How have you heard God's voice today?

Dear Parents and Caregivers

Here are some ideas for nurturing your child's prayer life:

● **Pray yourself!** When we do this, we witness to our children that prayer is important for everyone.

● **Introduce children to different types of prayer so that they understand that prayer is not just about asking for things:** For young children, begin by introducing the following three types of prayer: adoration – praising God; thanksgiving – giving thanks for what God has done for us; and petition – asking for God's help, guidance and forgiveness for ourselves and other people.

● **Introduce a variety of prayer forms:** Just as there are various learning styles, there are many prayer styles.

If your child is a visual learner, try …
… praying with art. Display religious images in your home – pictures, crucifixes, statues. Decorate for the liturgical seasons. Surround your child with religious images that reflect his or her cultural identity. Actively seek out diverse images so they can see the face of Christ in people of any size, shape or form. Use images of Mary holding Jesus or of the Guardian Angel to comfort fearful children.

If your child is an auditory learner, try …
… praying with music. Play a religious song before bed or before leaving in the morning to help your child pray "without ceasing" all day. Sing grace before meals.
… praying with story. Read Bible stories or the lives of the saints and finish with a prayer derived from the story.

If your child is a physical learner, try …
… journalling. Have them use a beautiful book to signify the sacredness of their writing. Use prayer starters such as *I am thankful for …, I am sorry for …, I need help with …, I saw you today, God, when …*
… praying with movement and ritual. Younger children need to move. Incorporate rituals into your prayer by making the sign of the cross, folding your hands and bowing your heads, using rosary beads, lighting candles, sprinkling holy water, changing your posture from kneeling to standing to sitting. Sing religious songs that have accompanying actions. Sprinkle children with holy water when they leave the house. Bless your house. Bless family pets on the Feast of St. Francis.

Meditate: Have children sit in silence for one minute each night before bed. Begin with the sign of the cross and then say, "Speak, Lord, I am listening." Remind children that God always has something good to say to them, such as "You are wonderful. Thanks for trying so hard." Explain that often God just wants to be with us in the quiet.

Use both memorized prayers and spontaneous prayers: Teach children to speak with Jesus from their heart as they would speak to a friend. Use children's prayer books to help them formulate prayers. Also teach them the favourite prayers of the church: the Lord's Prayer (Our Father), Hail Mary, Glory Be and a grace before meals. As they get older, they can learn the Apostles' Creed, Confiteor (I confess) and Prayer of St. Francis.

Pray at mealtime, bedtime and each morning: St. Paul tells us to pray always. To ensure that we engage in constant conversation with God, we can bookend our days with prayerful pauses. We can pray with thanks each time we gather for meals.

Pray for others: We help our children become generous and self-giving when we teach them to pray for others. Ask your children who needs prayers and include their names in a prayer at mealtime or bedtime. Point out stories in the news of people who need prayers. Light a votive candle after Mass for people in need. Teach children to make the sign of the cross and say a prayer when they hear a siren and to pray for the dead when they pass a cemetery.

Attend Sunday Mass: The Eucharist is the source and summit of our spiritual life and the place where our prayer life finds root. Sing songs from Mass for home prayer. Read the Sunday readings at home during the week. Take holy water from the baptismal font to use for prayer at home. Pray the same intentions from Sunday's Prayer of the Faithful at home.

By nurturing a prayer life in your child at a young age, you are giving them a gift that will last a lifetime! You are giving them tools they need to be people of gratitude in times of joy and people of strength in times of sorrow. Amen!

Christine Way Skinner has been a parish catechist for 24 years. She has a Master of Divinity from Harvard Divinity School and is the author of *Jesus Invites Me to the Feast: My First Eucharist Journal* (Liguori). When she is not trying to find inclusive, compelling and creative ways to pass on the Catholic Church's tradition, Christine enjoys reading, art, gardening and trying to convince her husband, Michael, and their house full of children that they really do love playing board games with her.

Céleste Gagnon is a full-time illustrator and designer. Over the last 15 years, Céleste has worked on many projects, including books, magazines, novel covers, merchandise, clothing, and fabric design. She loves what she does and the variety of work that comes with being an illustrator. When she is not working, Céleste likes reading, hiking and enjoying nature with her husband and their two young children.